Why Does Money Matter?

Rachel Eagen

 Crabtree Publishing Company
www.crabtreebooks.com

Money $ense

An Introduction to Financial Literacy

Author: Rachel Eagen

Series research and development: Reagan Miller

Editors: Reagan Miller and Janine Deschenes

Designer: Tammy McGarr

Photo research: Tammy McGarr and Crystal Sikkens

Proofreader: Petrice Custance

Prepress technician: Samara Parent

Print and production coordinator: Katherine Berti

Photographs

iStock: ©Steve Debenport: page 16

Shutterstock: ©Fat Jackey: page 5 (top right); ©testing: page 9;
    ©MinhHue: page 19

Thinkstock: title page (right)

All other images from Shutterstock

Library and Archives Canada Cataloguing in Publication

Eagen, Rachel, 1979-, author
    Why does money matter? / Rachel Eagen.

(Money sense : an introduction to financial literacy)
Includes index.
Issued also in electronic format.
ISBN 978-0-7787-2666-1 (hardback).--
ISBN 978-0-7787-2670-8 (paperback).--
ISBN 978-1-4271-1802-8 (html)

    1. Finance, Personal--Juvenile literature. 2. Financial security--
Juvenile literature. I. Title.

HG179.E2211 2016   j332.024   C2016-904172-7
                                            C2016-904173-5

Library of Congress Cataloging-in-Publication Data

CIP available at the Library of Congress

Crabtree Publishing Company

www.crabtreebooks.com   1-800-387-7650

Printed in Canada/082016/TL20160715

Published in Canada
Crabtree Publishing
616 Welland Ave.
St. Catharines, Ontario
L2M 5V6

Published in the United States
Crabtree Publishing
PMB 59051
350 Fifth Avenue, 59th Floor
New York, New York 10118

Published in the United Kingdom
Crabtree Publishing
Maritime House
Basin Road North, Hove
BN41 1WR

Published in Australia
Crabtree Publishing
3 Charles Street
Coburg North
VIC 3058

Table of Contents

What is Money?

In the past, it was common for people to **trade**, or exchange, things they had with other people to get new things. This is called **bartering**. For example, a farmer might give a builder potatoes in exchange for the building materials to fix his barn. Some people still use bartering today but most people trade money for things.

Money has value

Money includes the coins and bills we use to buy things. Coins and bills have different **values**, or how much something is worth. Coins and bills are stamped with numbers to show how much they are worth.

This coin is called a nickel. It is worth five cents.

Coins are small, flat pieces of metal.

This bill is worth one dollar.

Bills are made from paper.

Money Around the World

Currency is another word for money. It describes the money used in a country. Most countries have their own currencies. In fact, there are more than 160 different currencies around the world! You can learn about a country by looking at its currency. Bills and coins often have pictures showing important people, places, and events in that country.

Make "cents" of it!

This picture shows a twenty dollar bill from Fiji. What can you learn about Fiji by looking at this bill?

Different types, different names

Different types of currency have different names. The currencies used in the United States, Canada, and Australia, are called dollars. The United States has a one-dollar bill. Canada has a one-dollar coin called a loonie. People who live in countries in the **European Union** use euros. In the **United Kingdom** the currency is called the pound. The currency in Japan is called the yen.

Canadian loonie

euro

yen

pound

American one dollar bill

7

Why Money Matters

People around the world use money to pay for the things they **need**. Everyone has the same basic needs. A need is something people must have to survive. A place to live, food, water, and clothing are needs. The things we need cost money. People use money to pay for their needs.

This man is using euros to pay for food at a supermarket in Italy.

8

Different wants

People also use money to pay for things they **want**. A want is something people would like to have but they can live without. Wants include things like computers, family vacations, and toys. People have different wants depending on their interests.

These families are shopping at a Lego store in China. If they buy something at this store, will they be using money to pay for a need or a want?

Make "**cents**" of it!

Make a list of your wants and needs. Share your list with a friend. How many of your needs are the same? How many of your wants are the same?

9

Earning Money

A person **earns** money by working at a **job**. The money a person earns is called **income**. People go to school to learn the skills they must have for a job.

This woman earns money by working in a bakery.

Teachers work in schools. They help children learn.

Kids can earn, too

Kids can work to help out at home. Some kids earn an **allowance** for doing jobs such as washing dishes, walking the dog, and raking leaves.

These children are working hard to earn their allowance.

11

Spending Money

People work hard to earn money.

So what do they do with it once they have it?

People spend the money they earn on the **goods** and **services** they need and want. Goods are things that people can hold and touch, such as food and clothing. Services are work people do for others in exchange for money. People spend money on services such as visiting a doctor, getting a haircut, and swimming lessons.

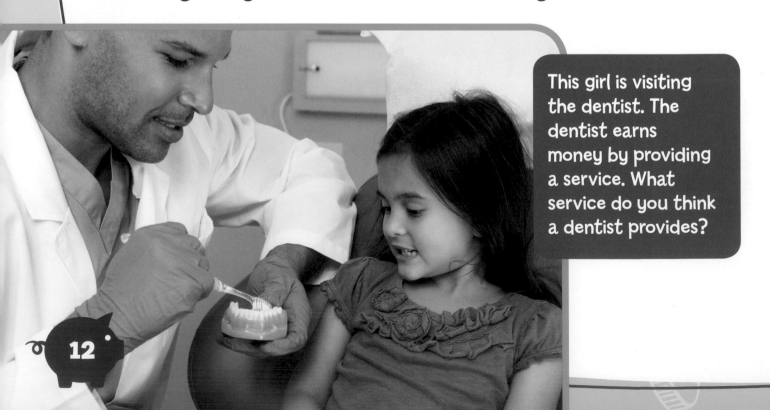

This girl is visiting the dentist. The dentist earns money by providing a service. What service do you think a dentist provides?

Money planning

Many people use a **budget** to help them make good money choices. A budget is a plan to track how money is spent and saved. People should first spend their money to get the things they need. If there is money leftover after their needs are met, people may then choose to spend it on things they want.

 Make "**cents**" of it!

Imagine you are in charge of your family's budget. Which goods and services would you spend your money on first? What would you buy only if you had money left over? Explain your thinking.

13

Saving Money

People try to save money for different reasons. Some people save money to pay for something that costs a lot, such as a new car or family vacation. People also save money for **emergencies**. Emergencies may include losing a job, car repairs, or other unplanned events.

People also save money to pay for things that will happen in the future. This family is saving money to pay for their daughter to go to college.

Money in the Bank

A **bank** is a business that helps people keep their money safe. People keep their money in **bank accounts**. They can put money in or take money out when they need it.

Kids can save money in bank accounts, too. Ask a parent if you can join them the next time they visit the bank.

15

Sharing Money

Some people choose to share some of the money they earn with others in need. One way to do this is to **donate**, or give, money to **charities**. A charity is an organization that raises money to provide help in the **community**, and to help people or animals in need. For example, some charities work to keep the **environment** clean. Other charities may help care for animals in need of homes.

Some charities use money to buy food for people who do not have enough money for food.

Giving feels good

Donating money helps people feel **grateful**, or thankful, for what they have. It feels good to help support a charity that is important. to you.

Instead of getting birthday gifts, some people choose to donate the money to help others. This boy is donating his birthday money to a children's hospital.

Kids for a Cause

Most kids do not have a lot of their own money to donate. This does not mean you cannot help others! Anyone can give their time and talent to raise money to help those in need. Some kid-friendly ideas include setting up lemonade stands, hosting bake sales, or selling artwork and crafts. Talk to an adult first. They can help you decide the best way to raise money to help others.

These kids will donate the money from their bake sale to the animal shelter in their community. An animal shelter is a place that cares for lost animals.

Every penny and every minute of your time can help! These children are raising money by running in a race called the "Run for Education." The money they raise will help build new schools in their country of Vietnam.

Good Money Choices

Now you know the ways people use money and why it matters to people around the world. People earn money to spend on things they need and want, save for the future, and to share and help others.

SAVE

SPEND

SHARE

Spend, Save, and Share

Learning how to make good money choices is an important skill you will use your whole life. It is never too early to start!

You can start by thinking carefully, and planning how you will use any money you earn or receive as a gift.

How will you spend, save, and share your money?

Make "cents" of it!

Some people use a chart like the one shown here to help them make good money choices. This chart will help you plan ahead and track how much money you spend, how much you save, and how much you may want to share. People use their money in the ways that work best for them. Talk to your parents about the money choices they make.

Spend

Description	Total

Save

Description	Total

Share

Description	Total

Learning More

Books

Burnstein, John. *Dollars and Sense: Developing Good Money Habits.* Slim Goodbody's Life Skills 101. Crabtree Publishing Company, 2011.

Schuh, Mari. *Types of Money*. Blastoff! Readers: Money Matters. Bellweather Media, 2016.

Schuh, Mari. *Money Matters: Earning Money*. Blastoff! Readers: Money Matters. Bellweather Media, 2016.

Websites

This link highlights currencies of the world and includes images of coins and bills used in different countries.
www.mathsisfun.com/money/currency.html

This site helps reinforce early money management skills using a three jar approach for spending, saving, and sharing money. An adult must create a free account for a child.
www.threejars.com

Words to Know

Note: Some boldfaced words are defined where they appear in the book.

allowance (uh-LOU-uhns) noun Money paid regularly to a child for specific work or chores

bank account (bangk uh-KOUNT) noun A record of money held at a bank for safe keeping

community (kuh-MYOO-ni-tee) noun A place where people live, work, and play

donate (DOH-neyt) verb To give something as a gift to help others

earn (urn) verb To gain by working

emergency (ih-MUR-juh n-see) noun Something that happens unexpectedly and needs attention right away

environment (en-VAHY-ruhn-muhnt) noun Everything that is around you, such as the soil and climate

European Union (yoor-uh-PEE-uhn YOON-yuhn) noun A group of over 25 countries in Europe, including France and Italy, who share a currency

job (job) noun A task done for a set amount of money

need (need) noun Something a person must have to be healthy and safe

United Kingdom (yoo-NAHY-tid KING-duhm) noun A group of countries that share a currency; includes England, Scotland, Wales, and Northern Ireland

want (wont) noun Something a person would like to have but does not need

A noun is a person, place, or thing.

A verb is an action word that tells you what someone or something does.

23

Index

About the Author

Rachel Eagen studied Creative Writing and English Literature at university. Now, she edits and writes books for a living. She is the author of 17 other books for children and youth. She plans to put the money she earned from writing this book into her what-if fund.